a gift from
greensboro

a poem by Quraysh Ali Lansana
illustrated by Skip Hill

penny
candy
BOOKS

Penny Candy Books
Oklahoma City & Savannah
© 2016 Penny Candy Books

This book is printed on paper certified to the environmental and
FSC social standards of the Forest Stewardship Council™ (FSC®).

Design: Shanna Compton, shannacompton.com

"A Gift from Greensboro" under the title "The Woolworth's Poem" was
first published in *Southside Rain* (Third World Press, January 2000) and
again in *The Walmart Republic* (Mongrel Empire Press, September 2014).

Photo of Quraysh Ali Lansana by Alan Tarin
Photo of Skip Hill by Doug Hill

20 19 18 17 16   1 2 3 4 5
ISBN-13: 978-0-9972219-1-6

Books for the kid in *all* of us.
www.pennycandybooks.com

For Russ and Tod

we rode
summer on
ten speeds

bike routes to
the courthouse lawn

EL GREENE
AJOR GENERAL IN
STERN ARMY   HAR

where parking meter hitching posts
lined melting,
technicolor
days

we knew every corner
of that department store

from the bird droppings
in the basement

to the scent
of musty popcorn

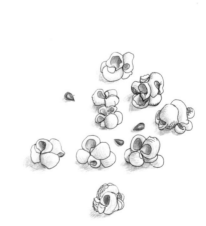

we dared lunch counters innocently
we laughed in the face of history

him, golden locked and chubby nosed
me, bubbling hot fudge

EVERYTHING MUST GO
70% OFF

now the parakeets and
canaries are no more

silence
    creeps the
ratchety escalator

those fat, pasty,
sandwich fingers

work now in
snaptight kitchens
across town,

their tenderness lost

on the last day of business
before it became a museum

after he grew up
but before he passed

he visited

WOOLWORTH'S

and bought me a coffee mug

he sat where freedom's students
wore ketchup and abuse

in a North Carolina
        before Michael Jordan

he sat once again
    where we used to sit

it is a simple mug

it meant
a lot to him
to give it to me

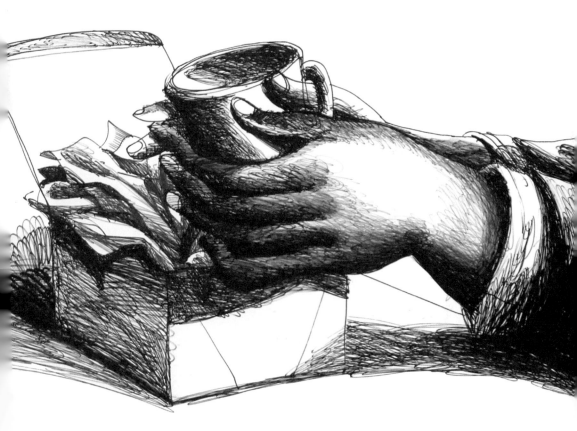

it means a lot to me to have it

A Gift from Greensboro

1

we rode summer on ten speeds
bike routes to the courthouse lawn

where parking meter hitching posts
lined melting, technicolor days

2

we knew every corner
of that department store

from the bird droppings in the basement
to the scent of musty popcorn

3

we dared lunch counters innocently
we laughed in the face of history

him, golden locked and chubby nosed
me, bubbling hot fudge

4

now the parakeets and canaries are no more
silence creeps the ratchety escalator

those fat, pasty, sandwich fingers
work now in snaptight kitchens
across town, their tenderness lost

5
on the last day of business
before it became a museum

after he grew up
but before he passed

he visited Woolworth's
and bought me a coffee mug

he sat where freedom's students
wore ketchup and abuse
in a North Carolina before Michael Jordan

he sat once again
where we used to sit

6
it is a simple mug

it meant a lot to him to give it to me

it means a lot to me to have it

The author & his childhood friends, as adults
From left to right: Tod, Quraysh, Russ

Author's Note

Russ and I first met on the basketball court at the Armory in Enid, Oklahoma. Three years later, in 1975, we were reunited at Garfield Elementary when my school, Roosevelt Elementary, was closed due to desegregation. Before the schools were combined, most of the kids at Roosevelt had been African American, and most of the kids at Garfield had been White. We had gone to different schools because of the color of our skin and the neighborhoods in which we lived.

The law that ended this separation of African Americans and White Americans is called **the Civil Rights Act of 1964,** enacted the year we were born. Some states, including Oklahoma, didn't agree with the law right away. These states continued to separate African Americans and Whites for as long as they could, and hoped the Federal Government wasn't watching. Some states got away with it for a very long time.

So, eleven years after the Civil Rights Act was passed, in a place that wasn't too happy about people of color going to the same stores, schools, and other places as Whites, Russ and I rode our bikes downtown to sit at the Woolworth's lunch counter to eat cheeseburgers and drink milkshakes. We didn't know that eleven years earlier it was against the law for me to sit next to my best friend at that counter. We didn't know there were people in the store, both shoppers and employees, that had a problem with us being there together. Yes, we knew about **Rev. Dr. Martin Luther King, Jr.** and I knew about **Ms. Clara Luper**, Oklahoma's most noted civil rights leader. But, we didn't think our small, happy little town had a problem. We were wrong. But, we were dreamers.

In 1958, Ms. Luper led young people from the NAACP Youth Council to Katz Drug Store in downtown Oklahoma City to stage the second sit-in protest in the United States. The sit-in led to the decision that Katz Drug Store would allow African Americans to eat at their lunch counter.

This sit-in protest in Oklahoma City happened a year and a half before the more well-known sit-in at the Woolworth's store in Greensboro, North Carolina, when on February 1, 1960, four African American college students started **the Greensboro Woolworth's sit-in**. Hundreds of people joined the four young men in their nonviolent protest, which lasted six months and resulted in the desegregation of the lunch counter.

That same store closed in 1993. On its last day of business my other best friend, Tod Lilburn, was sent there by the television station he worked for to shoot video for the nightly news. The decision to turn the store into a Civil Rights museum had not been made when he was there. Tod thought, as did many people in the area, that this important store was going to be torn down. He bought me the coffee mug as a symbol of our friendship. That even if the building was going to be demolished, our bond, a bond forged with love and laughter in the midst of intolerance and hate, would continue and thrive. The building sat vacant for eight years, but fortunately *the International Civil Rights Center and Museum* opened its doors in 2001, the same doors those four brave young men walked through in 1960.

Garfield Elementary School is now on the land where the Armory once stood. The place where Russ and I met a second time—when the schools in Enid were desegregated—is now at the same place we met the first time. Just as the Greensboro Woolworth's is now a place anyone can go to learn about the history of the Civil Rights Movement. Ms. Luper said, "My biggest job now is making white people understand that black history is white history. We cannot separate the two."

I wrote the poem in these pages to honor the memory of my two friends, but it's a fictionalized account set in Greensboro. While my two real-life friends are depicted by one boy in the poem, it captures the spirit of childhood friendships forged against the backdrop of history.

Quraysh Ali Lansana

QURAYSH ALI LANSANA loves to read, write, and imagine. His active imagination often results in books, events, and classroom lesson plans. Known by many as "Q," he has written eight poetry books, three textbooks, three children's books, and has co-written a book to help teachers teach poetry. Q has also edited eight anthologies of literature. He loves making books, studying history and politics, and learning about different cultures. Q also loves music, art, learning, and laughing.

Q loves to teach, and he has taught in elementary schools, high schools, and universities in Chicago, where he lives, and across the country. He teaches poetry and hip-hop at the School of the Art Institute of Chicago, across the street from the famous museum with the lions out front. Years ago, Q taught at the Juilliard School in New York City, and was Director of the Gwendolyn Brooks Center for Black Literature and Creative Writing at Chicago State University from 2002–2011, where he was also Associate Professor of English/Creative Writing until 2014. Q's favorite writers are Gwendolyn Brooks, Lucille Clifton, and James Baldwin.

SKIP HILL's body of art is comprised of illustrations, murals, collage paintings, and drawings that weave a rich tapestry of aesthetic styles, languages and philosophies rooted in cultures around the world. He explores images and forms from cultural sources as diverse as comic books, Folk art, Japanese Ukiyo-e prints, Graffiti, and European Art History to produce an art that embraces the viewer in a visually engaging experience.

Skip's early inspirations for making art were established in childhood through a love of reading and when his father introduced him to the work of artist Romare Bearden. Beyond his artistic innovations, Bearden's activism and commitment to the Civil Rights Movement has influenced Skip's commitment to using art and art education as a vehicle for affirming positive personal and social change.

That early inspiration is at the heart of Skip's process and in every line of the illustrations for *A Gift from Greensboro*.